AMAZING HISTORY

MUMMIES

John Malam

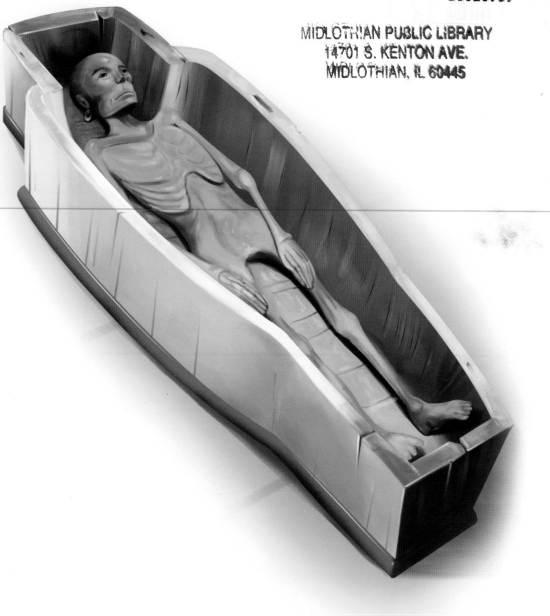

Smart Apple Media

Published by Smart Apple Media
2140 Howard Drive West
North Mankato, MN 56003

Created by Q2A Media
Series Editor: Jean Coppendale
Designers: Diksha Khatri, Ashita Murgai
Picture Researchers: Lalit Dalal, Jyoti Sachdev
Illustrators: Hemant Arya, Adil A Siddiqui, Amir Khan, Manish Prasad, Prashant Jogi, Subhash Vohra

Printed in China

Library of Congress Cataloging-in-Publication Data

Malam, John, 1957–
Mummies / by John Malam.
p. cm. — (Amazing history)
Includes index.
ISBN 978-1-59920-106-1
1. Mummies–Juvenile literature. I. Title.

GT3340.M35 2007
393'.3–dc22   2007014723

First Edition

9 8 7 6 5 4 3 2 1

Contents

What is a mummy?

A mummy is the **preserved** body of a dead person or an animal. The bones still have skin and flesh on them, the guts might be inside the body, and the hair and nails are still there.

Nature's own mummies

Some mummies are made by nature. These **natural mummies** have been preserved by accident. People have found them in **peat** bogs, hot deserts, dry caves, and in **glaciers** and frozen ground. Under these conditions, the process of decay is stopped, and instead of the body's soft parts rotting away, they survive for tens, hundreds, or thousands of years.

HOT SPOTS

One of the world's oldest mummies is a natural mummy—a man who died more than 5,000 years ago, whose body was kept safe inside a glacier (see page 16 for his story).

This body became a natural mummy as it slowly dried out in Peru, South America.

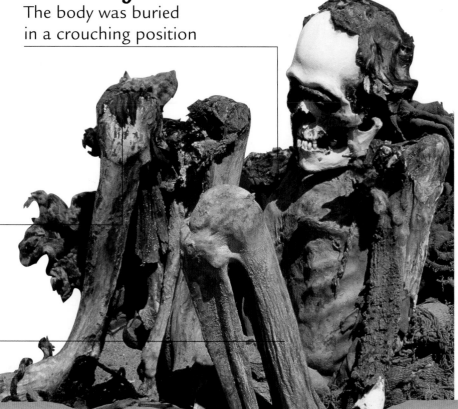

Crouching
The body was buried in a crouching position

Old bones
This person died about 1,500 years ago

Skin
Dried skin covers the bones

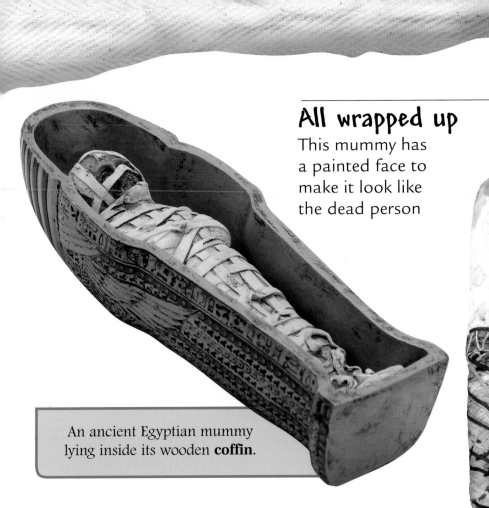

An ancient Egyptian mummy lying inside its wooden **coffin**.

Man-made mummies

Artificial mummies are ones made by people. The most famous were made by the ancient Egyptians, who made mummies for almost 4,000 years. The ancient Egyptians were not the world's only mummy-makers. People have also made mummies in South America, on the Canary Islands in the Atlantic Ocean, and on islands in the Pacific Ocean. Even the dead leaders of some modern-day countries have had their bodies mummified!

The mummy of an Egyptian person, who died about 3,000 years ago.

5

The first mummies

The world's first artificial mummies look like strange, black dolls. These mummies were made by people who lived along the coast of northern Chile, in South America.

SOUTH AMERICA

Chile

Human hair
Wig of long, black human hair

Coat of mud
The mummy was covered in mud that cracked and flaked

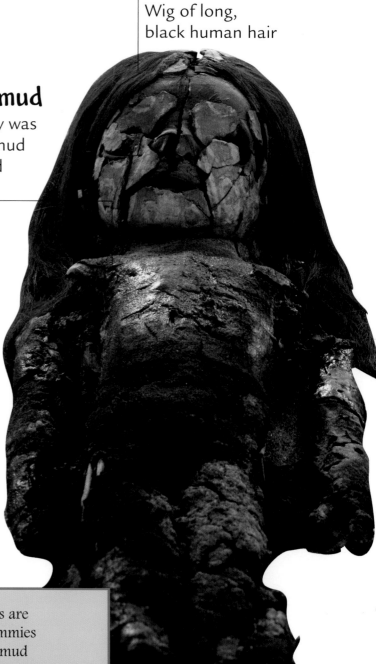

Black mummies

In 1983, an amazing discovery was made. Workers digging in Chile found some gruesome black figures with long human hair. The figures were covered in black, cracked mud, and instead of bones, they had sticks jutting out from their skin. The workers had uncovered an ancient cemetery filled with 100 famous Black Mummies of Chinchorro.

Chinchorro mummies are often called Black Mummies because of the black mud used to cover them.

Body builders

The Chinchorro mummies are special because of how they were made. The mummy-makers pulled the body apart and then put it back together again. The head, arms, and legs of the dead person were cut off, and the brain was taken out. The insides were removed, and the flesh was sliced from the bones. The skin and bones were left to dry. When the bones were dry, the skeleton was rebuilt.

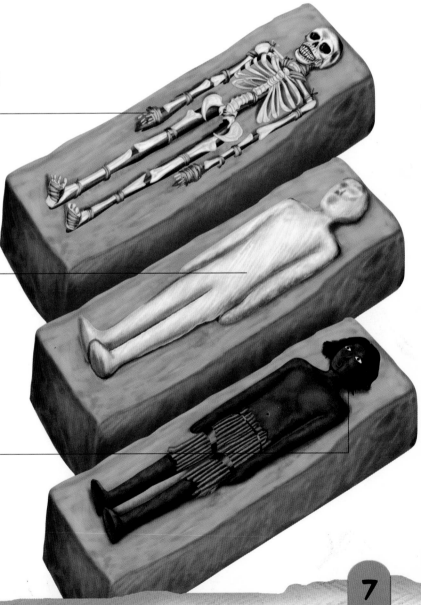

Tied to sticks

Sticks were tied to the arm, leg, and spine bones to hold the skeleton together

Covered in mud

Mud was spread over the skeleton and molded to build a body shape

Face and skin added

Real face skin was put back and patches of body skin and a wig of human hair were added

The finished mummy was painted black. Then it was buried in the ground.

Mummies of ancient Egypt

In ancient Egypt, bodies buried in the sand became mummies after many years. This gave the Egyptians the idea for making artificial mummies so that the dead could live in the **afterlife**.

Dried and shriveled

Egypt is a hot, dry country in North Africa and much of the land is sandy desert. Egypt's dead were buried in pits in the hot desert. Very slowly, over many years, their bodies dried out and shriveled until their skin was hard and tight. These natural mummies are about 6,000 years old.

Egypt

AFRICA

This natural mummy from the desert of Egypt was buried with things for him to use in the afterlife.

Burial pit
The dead were buried with pots and other things they might need in the afterlife

Flesh and bone
The skin dried and shriveled to the bone

Face mask
A mask covered the face to keep evil from entering the body

Lucky charms
Amulets, which were similar to lucky charms, were placed between the **linen** wrappings

Linen strips
The mummy was wrapped in thin strips of linen, which have begun to rot away

An ancient Egyptian mummy of King Amenemhat I.

To live forever

The ancient Egyptians probably started making mummies after they discovered that the bodies buried in the desert still looked like people—not piles of old bones. The ancient Egyptians believed that a person could live forever in the afterlife, as long as their body was saved. This meant that bodies had to be preserved by being mummified, so they could reach the afterlife. Ancient Egypt's first artificial mummies were made about 5,400 years ago.

HOT SPOTS

The ancient Egyptians believed that, after death, people went to another world—the afterlife— and lived again. They needed to take clothes and food with them.

Making mummies

Making a mummy in ancient Egypt was a messy, smelly job. It took about 70 days for the mummy-makers, or **embalmers**, to turn a dead body into a mummy.

The mummy-makers used their bare hands, hooks, and knives to pull out the dead person's organs.

Slippery insides

Inside an open-air tent, a team of embalmers worked quickly to take the slippery lungs, liver, intestines, and stomach out of the body. They kept these **organs**. The brain was thrown away because they thought it was of no value to the person. The heart and kidneys were left inside the body. Then, a big pile of **natron** (salty crystals) was put over the body. Over the next 40 days, the body slowly dried out.

Cut open
A cut was made into the left side, for the organs to be taken out

Canopic jars
The organs were mummified and saved in **canopic jars**

Outer coffin

Pharaohs had a coffin within a coffin

Inner coffin

The coffin was covered in signs and spells to protect the mummy inside it

Mummy

The body was carefully wrapped in strips of linen

Amulets

Hundreds of lucky charms were hidden in the layers of linen

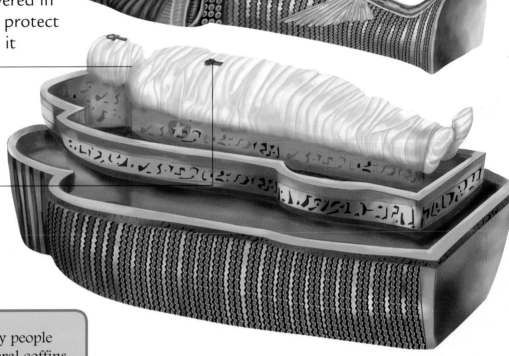

Pharaohs and wealthy people were buried inside several coffins that neatly fit together.

Wrapping and burying

The dried body was stuffed with clean rags, sawdust, and even mud to fill it out and give it a lifelike shape. A special plaque was put on the body to keep evil from getting inside. The skin was oiled, the face was painted, and a wig was put on the head. The mummy was then wrapped in narrow strips of white linen. Lucky charms, or amulets, were put between the layers. Last of all, the mummy was put in a coffin, ready to be buried.

HOT SPOTS

To get the brain out, a long metal hook was pushed up the left nostril and into the skull. The hook broke the brain into tiny pieces that were pulled out through the nose.

Bog bodies

The peat bogs of northern Europe might seem to be unlikely places to find mummies—but in their depths, searchers have found pickled people who look as if they fell asleep yesterday.

Tollund Man

More than 2,000 bog bodies have been found across northern Europe. The most famous bog body found in this region is Tollund Man, from Denmark. He was hanged, and his lifeless body was put into a bog where the peat preserved him—right down to the whiskers on his chin.

Most bodies found in bogs are between 1,500 and 2,500 years old. They are discovered in marshy areas where peat has formed.

Tollund Man may have been a criminal. The hangman's noose was left around his neck.

Only a hat

Tollund Man was naked, except for a leather hat

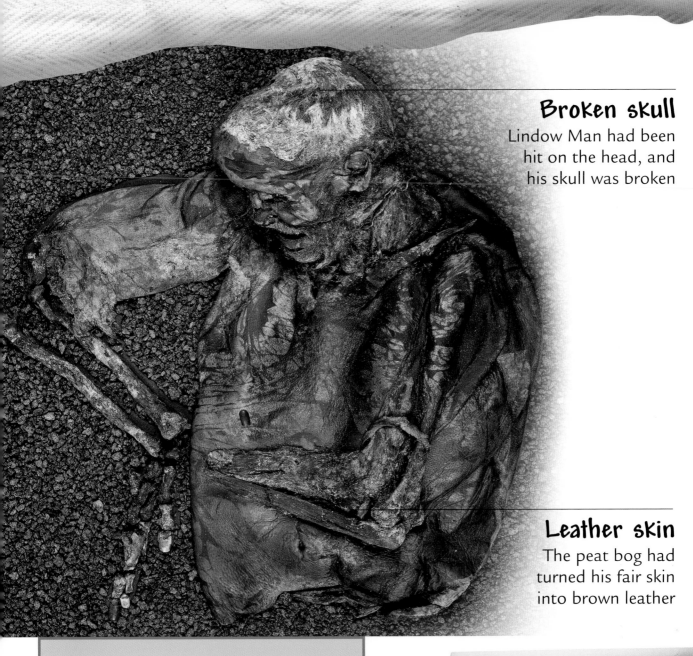

Broken skull
Lindow Man had been hit on the head, and his skull was broken

Leather skin
The peat bog had turned his fair skin into brown leather

Lindow Man was found when a peat-cutting machine sliced through his body.

Lindow Man

There is no oxygen or flesh-eating bacteria in a peat bog, so when a body sinks into one, its skin slowly turns to leather and its insides do not rot away. Lindow Man, from the United Kingdom (UK), was strangled, and his throat was cut before his body was dumped. He might have been a **sacrifice** to his gods.

HOT SPOTS
The top of Lindow Man's body was found first, and four years later, his left leg turned up. His right leg is either still in the bog or has been made into garden compost!

Frozen mummies

Well-preserved mummies have been found in the world's freezing places. These are natural, frozen mummies that have been preserved by ice or cold, dry air.

Family of mummies

About 500 years ago, a family of six Inuit women and two children died on Greenland. They were dressed in warm sealskin clothes and laid to rest on a rocky ledge. As time passed, the cold, dry Arctic air blew around the bodies, drying them out until they became mummies. They were found in 1972, by two brothers on a hunting trip.

The youngest of the Greenland mummies was a tiny six-month-old baby boy. At first, it was thought he was a doll, not a person.

Warm clothes
The baby's clothes were made from warm sealskin

The lost expedition

In 1845, two ships sailed from the UK in an attempt to cross the Arctic Ocean. The ships were never seen again, but 140 years later, the bodies of three of the doomed sailors were found buried in the frozen Arctic. Scientists opened their icy graves in 1984 and were amazed to see the men's bodies frozen in time, as if they had been in the ground for days, not years. Warm water was used to thaw them out. After examination, the graves were closed, leaving the Arctic to refreeze the **corpses**.

John Torrington, who took part in the Artic expedition. He died January 1, 1846, at the age of 20.

Frozen stiff

The frozen body of John Torrington inside its coffin

HOT SPOTS

William Braine, age 33, a member of the Arctic expedition was not buried right away. Scientists found out that his shoulders and chest had been nibbled by rats, which meant that his body must have been left lying around before it was put into the frozen ground.

The Ice Man

Mountains are dangerous places, so when a man's body was found in a glacier in northern Italy, police thought a hiker had died recently in a tragic accident. The truth is very different.

Europe's oldest mummy

The Ice Man's clothes and possessions were found near his body and these gave vital clues to his real age. He wore leather leggings, a goatskin coat, a bearskin hat, a grass cape, and leather shoes stuffed with grass. He had a copper ax, a bow and arrows, kindling for lighting a fire, a flint, and a wooden-framed backpack. He was more than 5,000 years old.

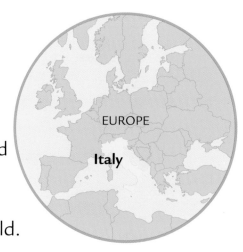

EUROPE

Italy

The Ice Man, photographed soon after he was removed from a glacier in 1991.

Icy grave
The Ice Man was found after a glacier melted

Attacked
An arrow hit him in the left shoulder

Death
He died on the mountain

Buried
Snow and ice covered his body

Archaeologists were stunned to discover that the Ice Man had lived 5,300 years ago, making him Europe's oldest mummy.

Was he murdered?

Why was he on the mountains? He might have been a shepherd, taking his flock to a summer grazing area or bringing them down for the winter. He could have been a hunter, which is why he had a bow and arrows. Whatever his job, a deep cut on his right hand shows he had been in a fight and an arrowhead lodged in his shoulder reveals that he was shot from behind. He may have fled to the mountains to escape from his attacker.

HOT SPOTS

A reporter invented the name Ötzi for the man, by mixing "Ötztal" (the region where the body was found) with "yeti," which is a legendary mountain creature.

Living mummies of Peru

Inca mummies, from Peru, South America, are some of the best-preserved in the world—and they are also the most mysterious. They were made between 500 and 1,000 years ago.

Talking to mummies

When an Inca emperor died, his body was mummified, dressed in fine clothes, and taken to a safe place. Servants brought food and drink to the mummy, as if he were still alive. On special occasions, the wrinkled mummies of Inca emperors were paraded through the streets. Because people saw that the emperors' bodies had not rotted away, they believed their rulers were still living among them and were able to protect and control their lives. Sometimes the mummies were carried through farmers' fields, in the hope that they would cause rain to fall on the crops.

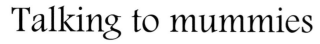

Peru   SOUTH AMERICA

Mummy bundle
The mummy was wrapped in sheets of cloth, making a **mummy bundle**

A **replica** of an Inca mummy is carried in a modern-day parade.

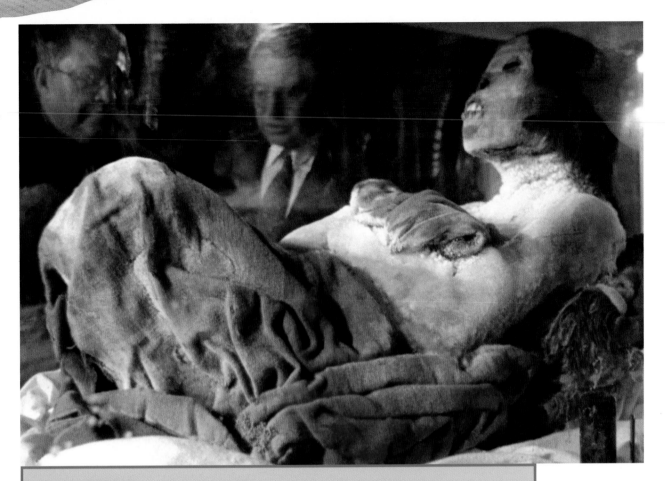

Children were the most precious gifts the Incas could offer their gods, and this is why the Ice Maiden was sacrificed to them.

Ice Maiden of the Andes

Five centuries ago, a teenage Inca girl was led to the top of Mount Ampato, a mountain that rises to 20,670 feet (6,300 m). It was a sacred mountain, and when the people reached the icy summit, the young girl was sacrificed to the Inca gods. She was buried with **offerings** of textiles, food, gold, and silver . . . and that was the last anyone saw of her until 1995, when her mummified body was discovered. The cold, icy conditions had dried and preserved her body.

HOT SPOTS

All the mummies of Inca emperors were lost or destroyed long ago, and no one living today has ever seen one.

The Palermo mummies

Did you know that mummies come from all around the world? They are everywhere, and you'll even see them standing around in old churches, especially on the island of Sicily.

Well-dressed mummies

A church at Palermo, on the Mediterranean island of Sicily, has thousands of mummies in its underground **vault**. Compared to other mummies, they are not very old—many are about 100 years old—but what's really interesting is what they look like. When a person died, they were dressed in their best clothes, then laid to rest in the dry vault.

EUROPE

Italy

Sicily

On display
This mummy was placed against the wall

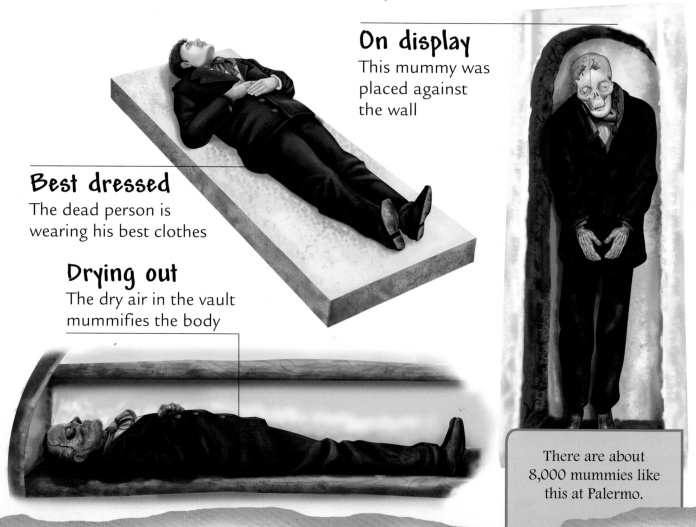

Best dressed
The dead person is wearing his best clothes

Drying out
The dry air in the vault mummifies the body

There are about 8,000 mummies like this at Palermo.

Mummy lineup

The dead people were left alone for their body fluids to evaporate. When they were as dry as a leaf, their dried-out corpses were propped up against a wall. The mummies were placed together in different poses, standing in a line. Some mummies have name tags to say who they are, but many are nameless.

They look like scary props from a haunted house, but these are the mummies of real people from Palermo, Sicily.

HOT SPOTS

Some of the best preserved mummies at Palermo are children. There are even two sitting together on a rocking chair.

This Palermo man died in the 1800s. His body has been mummified by the dry air.

Look inside a mummy

It's no wonder people are curious about mummies. Each one is a unique time capsule from whenever it was made, and when experts examine it, they unlock its secrets.

Unwrappers and unrollers

In the 1700s, mummies of ancient Egypt were crushed up to make medicine. Doctors thought the dust had the power to cure the sick. In recent times, ancient Egyptian mummies have been unwrapped by archaeologists, but unwrapping is destructive—once a mummy has been opened, it cannot be put back together again. Today, experts use **X-rays**, computer imaging, and tiny cameras to examine the inside and outside of a mummy without harming it.

A **CAT scanner** (Computerized Axial Tomography) examines a mummy without damaging it.

CAT scanner
Entrance to the scanner tunnel

Coffin
Inside this painted coffin is a mummy

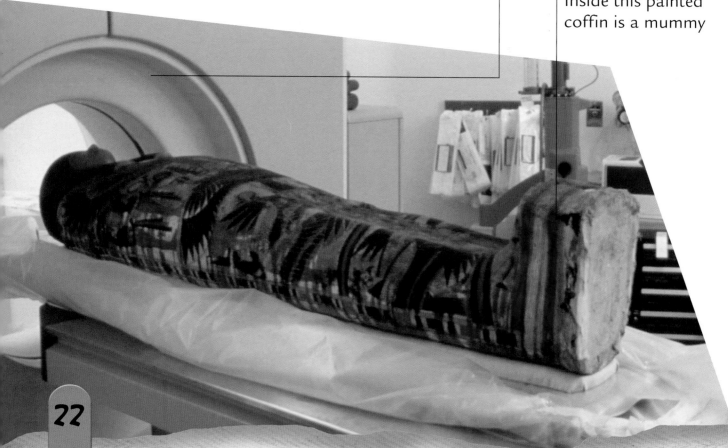

Putting the flesh back

At Manchester Museum in the UK, there is a mummy of an ancient Egyptian woman named Asru. Her dried-out body has been studied in detail. In particular, a CAT scan has given three-dimensional pictures of her body, from which an exact copy of her skull was made. A medical artist then rebuilt Asru's face over the model skull.

HOT SPOTS

*A tiny camera was put into Asru's mummy, and it found that she had a **tapeworm** in her lungs. It would have left her short of breath.*

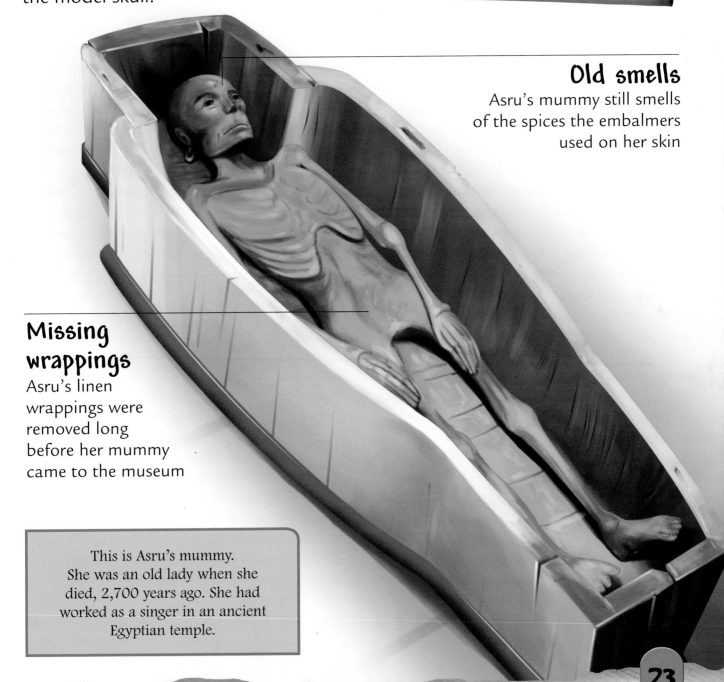

Old smells
Asru's mummy still smells of the spices the embalmers used on her skin

Missing wrappings
Asru's linen wrappings were removed long before her mummy came to the museum

This is Asru's mummy. She was an old lady when she died, 2,700 years ago. She had worked as a singer in an ancient Egyptian temple.

Animal mummies

It's not just humans that have ended up as mummies—animals have, too. Just like humans, some animal mummies have been made by people, and others have been made by nature.

Egyptian animals

The mummy-makers of ancient Egypt made millions of animal mummies. Some animal mummies were made in the same way as human mummies. But why did they do this to animals? Sometimes a pet cat, dog, or monkey was mummified so that it could go with its owner into the next life. Mummified birds or pieces of meat, were buried with dead people for food. Some animals, such as bulls, were made into mummies because they were sacred.

Small animals, such as birds and cats, were mummified quite quickly. They were dipped in hot **resin**, which dried hard, then they were wrapped up.

Cat mummy
This mummified cat has been very carefully wrapped

Animal embalmers in ancient Egypt were often frauds. Some crocodile "mummies" had no crocodiles inside them.

Best preserved
Baby Dima is the best
preserved mammoth
ever found

Hairy feet
Thick, red fur still
survives on its feet

Nature's animal mummies

Nature's most amazing animal mummies are
the deep-frozen mammoths of Siberia, in
northern Russia. Mammoths lived more than
10,000 years ago, when Earth was in the grip
of an **ice age**. These freezing conditions were
perfect for preserving the bodies of mammoths,
some of which have survived
to the present day.

HOT SPOTS

*The world's oldest mummy
is not a person but an
animal—an Edmontosaurus
dinosaur that died 65 million
years ago. It was found
in North America.*

This bird died in
a dry place, so its body
has been mummified.

Dead bird
This dead bird is
a natural mummy

A never-ending story

Who says mummies have to be old? They don't! You might be amazed to find out that the craft of mummy-making (and mummy-faking) is still used in the world today.

Modern-day mummies

In Moscow, visitors line up to see the preserved body of Vladimir Ilyich Lenin, the Russian leader who died in 1924. In Beijing, the crowds come to see the mummy of Mao Tse-tung, the leader of China who died in 1976. Both of these powerful men changed the course of their country's history, and after they died, people decided to save their bodies so that future generations could look at them.

The process used to preserve Lenin's body is top secret. Some people believe it hasn't worked, and that the "body" on display in Moscow is actually a dummy.

The Persian princess

It looked like a major discovery when the mummy of "Princess Rhodugune" was found in Pakistan. According to the writing on her coffin, she was the daughter of King Xerxes, who ruled Persia 2,500 years ago. The discovery made world headlines— but excitement turned to horror when the mummy was examined and found to be modern. Under all the wrappings was the body of a young woman who had been murdered and then mummified.

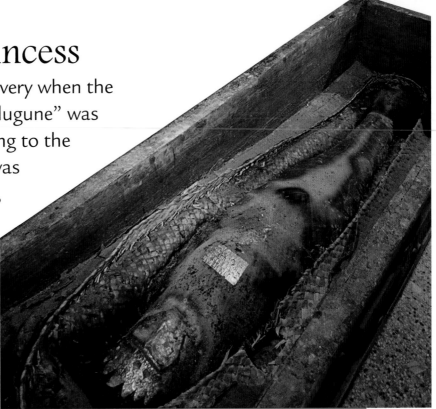

Princess Rhodugune, or the Persian Princess, is a modern murder victim whose killers tried to make a fortune by selling her mummy.

HOT SPOTS

There is a company that offers to make real human and animal mummies. A cat mummy costs $4,000, while a human mummy costs as much as $67,000!

This family pet dog was turned into a mummy by a company in the U.S.

Mummy mania

Mummies have been dead for many years, but they still find ways of being part of our lives today.

The mummy's curse

The ancient Egyptians believed in magic, which is why mummies were buried with spells. Some spells were **curses** to protect the mummies from tomb robbers. In 1922, the tomb of Tutankhamun was opened by Howard Carter and Lord Carnarvon. Shortly after, Carnarvon was bitten by a mosquito, the bite became infected, and he died. Newspapers said his death was due to the ancient curse, which was still working after thousands of years. One newspaper even printed a curse that was said to be found in the tomb: "They who enter this sacred tomb shall be visited by the wings of death." This is how today's idea of a "mummy's curse" began.

Howard Carter, the archaeologist who found Tutankhamun's tomb, examines the king's coffin.

Pharaoh
Tutankhamun was a king of Egypt

The inside of Tutankhamun's tomb today. His mummy lies inside its golden coffin, as it has for the last 3,300 years.

HOT SPOTS

The actor who played the mummy in the 1932 movie was Boris Karloff. On each day of filming, it took eight hours to dress him up to look like a moldy old mummy!

Movie mummies

The very first movie about a mummy was made in France in 1909. Since then, mummies have starred in many movies. One of the most famous—and scariest—was called *The Mummy*. It was made in 1932 and told the story of an ancient Egyptian mummy who came to life in the present day. More recently, blockbusters such as *The Mummy Returns* have thrilled audiences around the world. Modern mummy movies are packed with incredible special effects.

A poster for the classic horror film *The Mummy*. This black and white film was first shown in 1932. Even though it was made so long ago, it still scares people who see it today.

Glossary

afterlife The idea that, after a person dies, a part of them continues to exist in a new life after death.

amulets Lucky charms used to keep evil away.

archaeologists People who study the remains and monuments of the past.

artificial mummies Mummies that have been made by people.

canopic jars Four jars that held the mummified stomach, liver, lungs, and intestines of a person in ancient Egypt.

CAT scanner A machine that uses an electronic system called Computerized Axial Tomography (CAT) that can create pictures to show the inside of a living or dead body without cutting it open.

coffin A container, usually made from wood, in which a mummified body was placed.

corpses Dead bodies of people or animals.

curses Spells that cause evil or harm to someone or something.

embalmers People who preserve the dead body of a person or an animal so that it will not rot.

glaciers Large, slow-moving masses of ice.

ice age A period in Earth's history when the temperature was cooler than today and when ice sheets and glaciers covered more of the planet.

linen Cloth made from woven fibers of the flax plant.

mummy bundle A type of mummy from South America in which the mummy is wrapped in a big bundle of cloth.

natron A natural saltlike substance found in old lake beds in Egypt. It was used in the Egyptian mummification process because it dried out a body.

natural mummies Mummies that have been made by nature.

offerings Gifts to the gods, such as food, clothes, and sacrifices of animals and people.

organs Important parts of the body that have different jobs, such as the heart, brain, and lungs.

peat A soil-like substance in bogs, made from decayed vegetable matter.

pharaohs Rulers or god-kings of ancient Egypt.

preserved Kept in such a way as to stop decay, either naturally or deliberately.

replica An exact copy of something.

resin A very sticky substance that oozes from the bark of pine trees.

sacrifice Killing a person or animal as an offering to a god.

tapeworm A wormlike parasite that lives inside a living animal or human.

vault An underground room, often in a church.

X-rays Pictures of the bones inside a body.

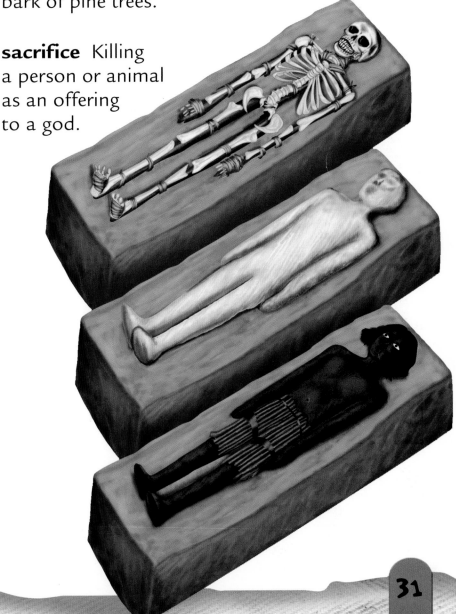

Index

Web sites

www.mummytombs.com/   A good place to start for anything about mummies.

www.animalmummies.com/   Animal mummies of ancient Egypt.

www.ancientegypt.co.uk/mummies/index.html   All about ancient Egyptian mummies from the British Museum.

www.archaeologiemuseum.it/index_ice.html   All about the Ice Man.